THE CHOIR OF ST. GEORGE'S

THE ROMANCE OF
ST. GEORGE'S CHAPEL
WINDSOR CASTLE

BY

HARRY W. BLACKBURNE, D.S.O., M.C.

(CANON OF WINDSOR, 1931–1934, AND CHAPLAIN TO
HIS LATE MAJESTY, KING GEORGE V)

WITH A FOREWORD
BY
THE DEAN OF WINDSOR
DR. BAILLIE, K.C.V.O.

RAPHAEL TUCK & SONS, L⊤ᴰ

LONDON . PARIS . NEW YORK

PRINTED IN ENGLAND

First Edition 1933
Second Edition (Revised) 1936

FOREWORD

IN this little book Canon Blackburne has written what he calls the Romance of St. George's Chapel. I suppose that means the human interest which has centred round the Chapel and left its marks upon it. Mr. St. John Hope wrote a monumental book on the architectural history of the building, but it barely touches on the human interest which surrounds it. There were, in the earlier 19th century, many books written on the romantic interest of the Castle, but they are too long, and do not mainly deal with the Chapel, so Canon Blackburne has, I think, performed a real service in giving to the public this little book.

We can't all be interested in architectural and archæological details, but everyone except the most unimaginative feels some little thrill when he finds in a building links with living men and women of the past.

A man who has sung Marbecke in his parish church feels some thrill when he thinks of Marbecke playing the organ here and writing his music, and when he knows more about that simple-hearted man. We like to think of Mr. Pepys sitting in a stall and having the music of the Anthem which Dr. Child had chosen especially for his edification brought to him. We like to remember Stanford almost every afternoon in the later part of the War sitting in the organ loft with the great Sir Walter, enjoying the music, and time after time writing new music to be sung by the choir he loved. We like to remember the majestic figure of Sir Walter himself, holding an almost sovereign place as the leader of church music in England for nearly half a century.

We can think of the great statesmen, warriors and courtiers who have been there : of the emperor Sigismund bringing the arms of St. George in their gorgeous setting ; of Charles the Bold of Burgundy leaving his Flemish shield of arms at the back of his stall ; of the King of Spain kneeling beside the King of England to swear a treaty before the Altar ; of the great Bedford, Governor of France ; of the tremendous figure of Charles Brandon, Duke of Suffolk, brother-in-law of King Henry VIII ; of the Chantries to pray for the souls of men who fell under the axe of Richard III ; of Shakespeare sauntering through the aisles and thinking over the Merry Wives of Windsor, which the choirboys were to act before the Queen ; of Horace Walpole lodging in a Canon's house and talking with enthusiasm of the Gothic architecture and the painted windows, and Fanny Burney bringing her delightful personality into the society in the Cloisters ; of good old George III trotting round to Communion at 8 o'clock in the morning, or coming to see the repairs and restorations which he lavished on St. George's—we still stand on the carpet he gave us in the Sanctuary. There are links with almost every side of life, and you can come back to St. George's from reading almost anything in literature and find some new associations.

But I think the most romantic thing of all is the great sword which hangs huge and stark behind the Altar, in

the Ambulatory. The sword of Edward III, the man
who stood at the moment in English history when Saxons
and Normans and Danes forgot their separate nationalities
and became Englishmen in the strenuous efforts of his
wars ; the man who founded the order to which the
Chapel belongs, and left his mark on English thought
and purpose in the idea of Chivalry which he enshrined
in the whole foundation.

We who live here and wander through its courts and
aisles at all hours are glad if we can do anything to help
others to feel something of the inspiration and happiness
that comes to us from this wonderful heritage.

ALBERT BAILLIE, Dean.

July, 1933.
  The Deanery,
    Windsor Castle.

PREFACE

MY thanks are due first and foremost to Mr. Alfred Evans, Verger of St. George's, and Mr. Lewis Stainton, Chapter Clerk; both are great lovers of the Chapel and from them I have obtained much information.

I should also like to thank the Dean for his delightful foreword; from him, Canon A. C. Deane, Sir Walford Davies, Dr. Fellowes and my son Hugh Blackburne I have received many helpful suggestions, for which I am most grateful.

Much of the information and some of the heraldic terms contained in the notes at the end of this book have been obtained from the *Manual of Heraldry* edited by Francis J. Grant, W.S., Lord Lyon King of Arms. I wish to thank Mr. John Grant, Edinburgh, for his kindness in allowing me to quote from this book.

Last but by no means least I must thank Mr. Owen Morshead for kindly correcting the proofs and for making many necessary alterations.

HARRY W. BLACKBURNE.

July, 1933.
   4 *The Cloisters,*
      Windsor Castle.

CONTENTS

LIST OF ILLUSTRATIONS

" They dreamed not of a perishable home
Who thus could build."

(WORDSWORTH, Ecclesiastical Sonnets, III, 45.)

" Give all thou canst; high Heaven rejects the lore
Of nicely-calculated less or more;
So deemed the man who fashioned for the sense
These lofty pillars, spread that branching roof
Self-poised, and scooped into ten thousand cells,
Where light and shade repose, where music dwells
Lingering—and wandering on as loath to die;
Like thoughts whose very sweetness yieldeth proof
That they were born for immortality."

(WORDSWORTH, On the Inside of King's College Chapel,
Cambridge.)

" Where through the long-drawn aisle and fretted vault
The pealing anthem swells the note of praise."

(GRAY, Elegy written in a Country Churchyard.)

THE ROMANCE OF
ST. GEORGE'S CHAPEL,
WINDSOR CASTLE

CHAPTER I

THE ROMANCE OF THE BUILDING

WAS it that King Edward IV wanted to build
a chapel to the greater glory of God which
would be worthy of the Knights of the Garter,
or because he, a Yorkist, wished to build a chapel even
more beautiful than that of Eton, which had been the
noble task of the Lancastrian King Henry VI? We
cannot tell.

What we do know is that, the ground to the west
of the chapel built by King Henry III in 1240 being
cleared, the work of building St. George's was begun in
June, 1475, under the supervision of Richard Beauchamp,
Bishop of Salisbury, cousin of the king.

Teynton stone was brought by river from the Cots-
wold village of Burford, timber from the neighbouring
villages of Upton, Farnham, and Sunninghill; and with
Thomas Canceller as clerk of the works, William Berke-
ey head carver, Henry Jenyngs head mason, and John
Tresilian head smith, the work began. The choir and
its aisles were the first parts of the chapel to be carried

up to their full height and roofed in, but only a portion of the choir aisles was vaulted in stone. The nave walls as far as the two western chapels reached the height of the window sills before the death of King Edward IV in 1483, and the canopied stalls in the choir were erected by 1485.

We can picture the men at work in the chapel, each party of workmen under the supervision of a master craftsman. John Tresilian, a Cornishman, with the help of his smiths, made those iron gates which are so greatly admired. These gates, which now stand in the Sanctuary, were intended for the tomb of his royal master, which was then in course of construction.

His attention was next directed to the locks on the doors of the chapel, which he made with such skill that to-day they are as good as when they were first fixed in the doors. If we examine the Elizabethan lock on the door between the choir and the nave we cannot fail to see, beautiful though it is, that it reveals less skill in craftsmanship than those made by John Tresilian.

While the smiths were at work, masons and wood-carvers were engaged at their special tasks. What care was taken can be seen in the beauty of the stone-work and the carving, which is unsurpassed. All this work, so beautifully designed and so marvellously carried out, reminds one that

> In the elder days of art,
>   Builders wrought with greatest care
> Each minute and unseen part ;
>   For the Gods see everywhere.
>
> (LONGFELLOW, " The Builders.")

TOMB OF KING EDWARD IV
John Tresilian's gates

During the short reign of King Richard III work on the chapel may have been continued, but no record of what was actually done is in existence. But after he was slain at the Field of Bosworth, and the Crown was picked up near a hawthorn tree and placed on the head of King Henry VII, the work was pressed on.

Under the supervision of Sir Reginald Braye and Christopher Urswick, of both of whom we shall have more to say later on, the nave was carried further westward so as to include two more chapels; and, the work on the walls being complete, the nave and transepts were roofed in as they are to-day. Bosses of great interest and beauty were carved on this magnificently vaulted roof. There can be seen among many others the Tudor portcullis, white and red roses interspersed, a boss in the centre signifying the hawthorn tree of Bosworth Field, the arms of Dean Urswick and of Canon Oxenbridge, and the arms and badge of Sir Reginald Braye. When this task was finished, and after the death of Sir Reginald Braye, the choir, which had before only a wooden roof, was vaulted in stone. On the outside, the King's Beasts were placed on the pinnacles. From the one print in existence it is impossible to give any description of these beasts; but we may conclude that, in accordance with the Tudor custom, the houses of York and Lancaster were represented in those strange animals with their heraldic shields. Both inside and outside, then, of this marvellous chapel, there were striking evidence that the Wars of the Roses had been brought to an end and both factions united under the rule of a Tudor king.

c

In 1510 the roof of the ambulatory behind the altar was panelled in stone, and so, thirty-five years from the beginning of the work, the chapel was completed except for the stone vaulting over the organ; this was added in 1528 by King Henry VIII, whose arms can be seen in the centre of the vaulting surrounded by the arms of the Knights of the Garter of that time. At the beginning of his reign King Henry VIII converted the chapel over King Edward IV's tomb into a royal pew, where Queen Catharine of Arragon could sit with her ladies and watch the ceremony of the installation of the Knights of the Garter. On the centre panels of the exquisitely carved wooden balcony are the badges of King Henry VIII and Queen Catharine. This royal pew was occupied frequently by Queen Victoria during her great reign, and from it she witnessed the wedding which brought such joy to the country, between the Prince of Wales and Princess Alexandra of Denmark.

On one occasion when the service was long and the chapel cold, Queen Victoria remarked on the kindness of the Prime Minister, Lord Melbourne, who made matters bearable by keeping up a good fire. The chapel is now well warmed with pipeless heating and the fireplace has been removed.

Let us stand inside the chapel, and as the eye follows those tall, graceful shafts to the vaulted roof, we see there the perpendicular style at its perfection. While on the continent Gothic architecture developed along decorated and flamboyant lines, we in this country produced the perpendicular, of which King's College Chapel at Cambridge, and Henry VII's Chapel at

Westminster are notable examples. Both are similar in style to St. George's Chapel, but this, by the width of its vaulted roof, can claim to be the boldest of the three. Is it unwarranted to suggest that the perpendicular style of architecture, with its long straight lines and its perfectly carried-out arches, marked the new line of thought that was beginning to take shape in England? Such sermons in stone speak, to all who have eyes to see, of the straightness of life and the honesty of purpose which began to mark the English character and which, if the English character is to live, must develop more and more as years go on. Let worshippers and sightseers catch the message that rings out from these stones, laid so gracefully and carried up so high; let them take this message home and try to live it out in their lives, in order that that which was once a pious dream may become a reality.

CHAPTER II

The Romance of the Sword

BEHIND the reredos there hangs a sword, the all-conquering sword of King Edward III, which hung over his stall in the original chapel of the Knights of the Garter when in 1347 that Most Noble Order was founded. But when the new chapel was built this sword in all probability hung above the altar. During the Commonwealth, when all other swords were stolen, it seems likely that this sword was hidden, and at the Restoration it was hung in the vestry.

In recent years it has been given a more worthy and fitting position. It hangs on the wall of the ambulatory to the east of the altar. Facing it, is the old 13th century door with its beautifully twisted ironwork. This was the west entrance to King Henry III's chapel, which was made by King Edward III into the chapel of the Knights of the Garter. Above the sword, cut out of the stone, is the white rose of York with the consecration cross in the centre.

The sword is emblematic of all for which this ancient order of chivalry stands. "No Order in Europe is so ancient, none so illustrious, for it exceeds in Majesty, honour and fame all Chivalrous Fraternities in the world."

King Edward III had, in his youth, seen the honour of England dragged in the dust. The power of the crown had fallen into unscrupulous and self-seeking hands, and his father, King Edward II, had been done to death in the dungeons of Berkeley Castle. King Edward III came to the throne determined to restore the prestige of England, and he called upon the nobility to help him in his task. Inspired by the ancient traditions of King Arthur and his Knights of the Round Table, he created this Order which ushered in the dawn of nobler days, and of which Shakespeare afterwards wrote :

"When first this Order was ordained, my Lords,
Knights of the Garter were of noble birth,
Valiant and virtuous, full of haughty courage,
Such as were grown to credit by the wars ;
Not fearing death, nor shrinking for distress,

SWORD OF KING EDWARD III
Rose of York above

But always resolute in most extremes.
He that is not furnished in this sort
Doth but usurp the sacred name of Knight,
Profaning this most Honourable Order."

From that day the kings and queens of England have placed themselves at the head of the Order, whose members pledge themselves to support the laws of God and of the realm, and to stand up for all that is noble, just, and true.

This is not the place to give any detailed account of all who were included in the foundation of this Order—this College, to use its ancient name,—with its Dean, Canons, Priest Vicars (Minor Canons), Lay Clerks, and Choristers. Mention, however, may be made of the Military Knights of Windsor. These Knights are selected on account of their distinguished service in the army; they receive a small income and are given houses within the castle walls, their main duty being to represent at the services the Knights of the Garter, who, being all men of affairs, are only able to attend the chapel services on special occasions. As, Sunday by Sunday, the Military Knights march into their seats, we are reminded not only of their distinguished military service but also of the ancient Order which they represent.

As we look again at this Sword of State and read the statutes of the Order of the Garter, we are struck by the close similarity between these rules and those laid down by General Baden-Powell when he instituted that other order of chivalry, the Boy Scouts' movement. The sword links the present with the past, and as bodies of Boy Scouts and Girl Guides visit the chapel, let them look at that sword with feelings of determination that they too will live up to the ideals of their Order, which, in its ever widening circles, is doing much to bring about a brother-hood among nations, and to establish peace and goodwill in all parts of the earth. St. George's Chapel might well be called the shrine of the Boy Scout movement, for it was built to commemorate those ideals for which the Scout movement stands to-day : " Not a sword but peace."

Perhaps the greatest of all the Romances of the Sword is that which is blazoned forth to all who raise their eyes and scan the bosses on the vaulted roof of the choir and nave. Everywhere are to be seen the White and the Red Rose, linked together by some other emblem or joined into one, so making the Tudor Rose. The tombs of the kings belonging to these two opposing factions, York and Lancaster, are now to be seen on each side of the altar ; King Edward IV, the Yorkist king, on the north side, and King Henry VI, the Lancastrian, on the south side. What tragedy lies around the life stories of these two kings ; what disaster to the country was brought by those sanguinary Wars of the Roses ! War to the death in all parts of the country, savage battles, ruthless executions, shameless treasons—" Not peace but a sword." But the tombs are linked together by the vaulted roof ; in the Tudor dynasty the two warring factions were united, for King Henry VII, whose mother was Lancastrian, married Elizabeth of York, and, for the time being, civil war was brought to an end. The vaulted roof with its bosses proclaims " Not a sword but peace."

OXENBRIDGE CHANTRY-CHAPEL

CHAPTER III

THE ROMANCE OF THE CHAPELS

THE first side chapel to be built and equipped was that at the south-east corner of the building. It now contains the monument of Edward Clinton, first Earl of Lincoln (1512-85), with his wife and children, and is called the Lincoln Chapel. In 1481 the bones of one John Shorne were brought from North Marston, where he was rector during the closing years of the 13th century. His memory was held in great veneration as a protector against ague, and the lines about him run as follows :—

> " Master John Shorne, gentleman born,
> Who conjured the Devil into a boot."

So great was his reputation as a healer of men that pilgrims from all over England used to visit his tomb. Unfortunately nothing is known of the nature of the shrine which contained the bones of the good rector, but we can picture the constant stream of pilgrims coming to this chapel, hoping either to obtain healing or to ward off the danger of that dire disease. King Edward IV hoped that by bringing the bones of John Shorne to Windsor he would draw away some of the pilgrims who flocked to the tomb of King Henry VI at Chertsey.

Opposite this chapel, where now there stands a copy of a black-letter Bible, known as a Treacle

Bible,[1] there used to be a manuscript copy of a Sarum Service Book. The inscription beneath it is still there, and runs as follows :—" Who laid this book here ? The Reverend Father in God Richard Beauchamp of the Diocese of Salisbury. And wherefore ? to this intent, that Priests and Ministers of God's Church may have the occupation thereof, saying Divine Service, and for all other that listen to say thereby their devotions. Asketh he any spiritual meed ? Yea, as much as Our Lord list to reward him for his good intent : praying any man whose duty or devotion is eased by this book, they will say for him this common orison, Dominie Jesus Christ, kneeling in the presence of this holy Cross ; for the which Reverend Father in God above-said hath granted of the treasure of the Church to every man 40 days of pardon."

The Cross mentioned is carved on the roof above. St. George's Chapel possessed a famous relic known as the " True Cross," said to be a portion of the Saviour's Cross. It belonged to the Princes of North Wales and was taken from them by King Edward I in 1283. King Edward III, on the foundation of the Order of the Garter, gave it to the chapel of the Order at Windsor, where it became the chief relic. It was moved into St. George's during the reign of King Edward IV, but in 1548 the back of it, which was of gold, was sold by the Chapter, and what became of the Cross itself is not known.

The two recumbent figures in alabaster now in the Lincoln Chapel are those of Edward, Earl of Lincoln,

---

[1] The Bishop's Bible, 1568, was so called from its rendering in Jeremiah VIII, 22, ' is there not tryacle in Gilead ', but the word tryacle was used in Bibles of an earlier date, as can be seen from Marbecke's Concordance, 1550.

and his third wife, Lady Elizabeth Fitzgerald. On the armour at the side of the knees is an anchor; he was Lord High Admiral of the Fleet of Queen Elizabeth. At his feet is a greyhound. The Lady Elizabeth has a Paris hood on her head, and the Fitzgerald ape at her feet. The seven daughters kneeling below are the children of the first and second wives.

Having started with the Lincoln Chapel, we will take the side chapels one by one in order, going from east to west, and then back from west to east.

THE OXENBRIDGE CHAPEL

Little is known of John Oxenbridge beyond the fact that he was Canon of St. George's from 1509–1522, and a liberal benefactor. We may assume that he undertook the supervision of the work done in the chapel during that part of the reign of King Henry VIII. The close similarity between this chapel and that on the other side makes it certain that the Oxenbridge Chapel must have been a copy of the one built to William, Lord Hastings. Over the door is a rebus of the founder's name, an Ox, the letter N, and a Bridge with water running under it.

The chapel was dedicated to St. John the Baptist, this dedication being borne out by the pictures of the saint painted on the back of the panels of the Garter Stalls :— (1) the Baptist preaching to Herod, who is clearly vexed by the sermon, (2) the executioner giving the head to the daughter of Herodias, (3) Salome carrying in the head to Herod. In this picture, over Herod's head, is a crystal globe. Crystal-gazing was at that time much in vogue, and

D

the artist wished to convey the idea that a horrible fate was hanging over Herod for having committed such an atrocious deed. The pictures bear the date 1522, and have always been attributed to a Flemish hand. Professor Tristram, however, when he cleaned and restored these paintings in 1932, gave it as his considered opinion that in all probability they were the work of an English artist trained in the Dutch or Flemish schools.

THE KING CHAPEL

Here lie the remains of Dr. Oliver King, Canon of Windsor and Registrar of the Order of the Garter in 1489, and later Bishop, first of Exeter and then of Bath and Wells. The inscriptions and devices on the walls are said to allude to a vision which came to Dr. King while he was at Bath and which led him to rebuild the Abbey Church there. It is said that he saw the Holy Trinity with angels ascending and descending by a ladder, near to which was an olive tree supporting a crown. The impression was so strong that the doctor thought he heard a voice which said, " let an Olive establish the Crown, and let a King restore the Church." It is supposed that the text " de sursum est " (it is from on high), refers to this vision. On the walls are also painted the motto, " ut discam " (that I may learn), a large chained book, and the picture of a book-marker formed of many-coloured strings and loosely tied in a knot.

On the floor of this chapel are the remains of a brass[1] bearing the name of William Mugge, the first Warden of the College in 1380, and two brasses with curious in-

[1] Transferred from the earlier Chapel.

BRAYE CHAPEL
Prince Imperial Cenotaph

scriptions dated 1630 and 1633, to the memory of Dorothy and William, the children of another Dr. King who was also a Canon of Windsor. How pathetic are the inscriptions around these little tombs, which, in a few words, tell the story of a tragedy that other parents know so well, of lives lent for a brief space and then taken home. In this chapel there is also kept a painted wooden font of the 17th century, about which nothing is known.

The panel of the Four Kings, as it is called, which faces this chapel, bears testimony to the cruelty of King Richard III. The panels, painted early in the 16th century, bear the portraits of four royal personages, to three of whom Dr. Oliver King acted as secretary—those, namely, of Prince Edward (son of King Henry VI), King Edward IV, King Henry VII, and, standing between the last two named, the pathetic figure of King Edward V, who, with his brother the Duke of York, was flung into the Tower and brutally murdered by the order of his uncle, King Richard III.

CHAPTER IV

THE ROMANCE OF THE CHAPELS (CONTINUED)

THE BRAYE CHAPEL

SIR REGINALD BRAYE was the knight who, on the field of Bosworth, picked up the crown that had fallen from the head of King Richard III and placed it on the head of King Henry VII. Not only was

Sir Reginald an illustrious warrior; he will also be always remembered as a famous architect and a liberal benefactor. Under his guidance the chapel was nearly finished. The frequent occurrence of his arms and his badge in the decoration of the nave and transepts of St. George's bears witness to his interest in and liberality to the work done under his supervision. His badge is the hemp-brake, a toothed instrument for bruising or crushing hemp.

He, together with his two friends, Dean Urswick and Dr. Oliver King, were great supporters of King Henry VII, as they had been of his mother the Lady Margaret. On Braye's death in 1502 his executors caused this portion of St. George's to be set apart as his chapel. He was a man of high character, who, being a fervent lover of public justice, did not fail to admonish the king when he did anything contrary to justice or equity.

The Braye Chapel is filled with other memorials, one to Giles Thomson, for thirteen years Dean of St. George's and afterwards Bishop of Gloucester. He was one of the eight scholars selected in 1607 for the task of making a new translation of the Gospels, Acts and Revelation, which was to form part of the Authorised Version, as it came to be called. He is represented holding in his hands a copy of this book.

Another memorial, executed in Purbeck marble, is an Altar Tomb containing the remains of Sir William Fitz-William, who died in 1551. The memorial to Sir Richard Wortley (d. 1603) is set in a framework of Della Robbia pottery; in each of the bays of this chapel there used to be more of this same beautiful ware. Yet another memorial is that of Dr. Brideoak, sometime headmaster of Manchester

RUTLAND CHAPEL
Manners' Tomb

Grammar School; he was successively Canon of Windsor, Dean of Salisbury and Bishop of Chichester. He suffered considerably during the Commonwealth, and died in 1678.

Coming to more recent times, there is a memorial to Prince Christian Victor (*d.* 1900), the eldest son of Prince Christian and Princess Helena (daughter of Queen Victoria). He died in Pretoria from fever contracted during the South African War and was buried there. In the centre of the chapel there is a white marble cenotaph of the Prince Imperial. He was the only son of Napoleon III and the Empress Eugénie, and was killed in the Zulu War in 1879. A prayer found written in his notebook is recorded on one side of the memorial; and on the other side a quotation from his will of which the following is a translation :—

"I die with sentiments of profound gratitude to Her Majesty The Queen of England, to all the Royal Family, and to the country where I have received during eight years such cordial hospitality."

As we look at that thrillingly handsome young figure we can understand the grief of his mother and that of Queen Victoria.

This memorial and the windows of this chapel, which have in them the letter "N" for Napoleon and the French eagle, were erected by subscription in France and England. The last memorial to be placed in this chapel is that of Edmund Verney Wyatt-Edgell; he was a descendant of Sir Reginald Braye, and his sword hangs over the memorial erected to his forbear.

THE BEAUFORT CHAPEL

(*Dedicated to the Blessed Virgin Mary*)

Here lie the effigies of Charles, Earl of Worcester, the last near relation of King Henry VII, and therefore the last of the great Lancastrians, and the Lady Elizabeth Herbert, his wife. The bronze grating round the tomb, one of the few pieces of foreign work in St. George's, was badly damaged during the Commonwealth, when part of it was sold; but later it was repaired by the Duke of Beaufort, the descendant of the Earl of Worcester, and what was wanting supplied. A year later, in 1699, on the death of the Duke, a huge marble monument was erected to his memory, but owing to its size it was removed to Badminton in 1874.

THE URSWICK CHAPEL

Dean Urswick may be called one of the great saints of St. George's. For a number of years, as Dean, he worked with Sir Reginald Braye in finishing the fabric. He was one of King Henry VII's close friends and was largely instrumental in bringing about the marriage of the King with Elizabeth of York, daughter of King Edward IV. Being a man of great piety and humility he refused all offers of ecclesiastical preferment, resigning the Deanery of St. George's and all his other preferments in 1505, and contenting himself with the charge of souls in the parish of Hackney, where he died and was buried in 1521.

Wherever his arms are cut in the stone of the vaulted roof the word "Misericordia" (have compassion), is included, and the closing words of the inscription on the wall above his chapel run as follows :—

"Oh God, who by thy only begotten Son didst redeem mankind, being incarnate of the Virgin's womb and having suffered death, deliver we beseech thee the souls of Henry VII and Christopher, and all those whom Christopher offended during life, from eternal death, and bring them to eternal life. Amen. God have mercy."

In 1824, King George IV having ordered that a memorial to his daughter Princess Charlotte was to be erected in the Urswick Chapel, the Chapter directed that the ancient screen of the chapel should be removed ; so, with the utmost care, it was put up in the south aisle of the choir, "the Chapter" so runs the entry, "being unwilling that a memorial to one of their former Deans and a principal promoter of the edifice of their noble Chapel should be lost." A marble monument of Princess Charlotte and her stillborn son, executed by Wyatt, was then erected. At the last restoration, 1920–1930, the screen which Dean Urswick had himself erected and which had been removed was restored to its old position. Two painted panels of wood, now in the Chapter Library, are all that is left of the contents of this chapel. Outside the chapel is the statue of Princess Charlotte's husband,

Prince Leopold of Saxe-Coburg, later first King of the Belgians, with whom Princess Charlotte spent one of the few happy years of her brief life. This statue was erected in 1879 by Queen Victoria in loving memory of that uncle on whose advice she relied during the earlier years of her reign.

THE RUTLAND CHAPEL

Though there is no direct mention of King Richard III in St. George's Chapel, his name has a sinister sound within its walls. In this Rutland Chapel, founded in 1481 by Sir Thomas St. Leger, the husband of Anne, Duchess of Exeter and sister of Edward IV, who died in 1475, there is a silver-gilt memorial plate erected to their memory. Sir Thomas St. Leger was summarily beheaded by King Richard III as a dangerous adversary.[1]

In the middle of the chapel there is a beautiful alabaster tomb of George Manners, Lord Roos, who died in 1513, and his wife Anne, daughter of the Duchess of Exeter. These were the grandparents of Sir John Manners, who eloped from Haddon Hall with Dorothy Vernon, and whose descendants became Dukes of Rutland.

This chapel is used for the week-day celebrations of the Holy Communion, and is reserved for prayer and meditation at all times when St. George's is open to the public.

[1] The crucifix at the top of the plate was damaged by the Cromwellian soldiers; it too has now been restored.

ST. GEORGE'S CHAPEL
South Front

Those who use it are thankful to the Dean (Dr. Baillie) for the beautiful restoration which he carried out in memory of his wife.

THE HASTINGS CHAPEL

This chapel strikes the same sinister note regarding King Richard III. William, Lord Hastings, who for more than twenty years had served as Chamberlain to King Edward IV, was beheaded by King Richard III in 1483. The story runs that little more than a month had passed since the death of King Edward IV when the Duke of Gloucester, entering the Council Chamber, charged Lord Hastings with designs upon his life, banging his hand upon the table. The room was immediately filled with soldiers. " I will not dine," said the Duke, " until they have brought me your head," and Lord Hastings was hurried to instant execution in the courtyard below.

The chapel, which is dedicated to St. Stephen, has in it some unique mediaeval paintings by an English artist which can be dated about 1490. The pictures give representations of the life of St. Stephen :—(1) preaching to a crowd of eager listeners, (2) brought before Herod, (3) stoned with English flints, while Saul sits in a corner holding the clothes of the stoners, (4) the soul of St. Stephen, as of a little child, presented to God in Heaven. The faces of the two false witnesses in the trial before Herod are most interesting, for they are covered with beads of perspiration, revealing the fact that " conscience doth make cowards of us all." Beneath the

E

panels are Latin inscriptions, which translated are as follows :—

1. He preaches thrift, He dies to live with honour, His doctrine checks and soothes the hearts of men.
2. Pursued by envy, suspected by Herod, wicked men accuse the holy Stephen.
3. Paul of his own accord holds the clothes of them that stone him.
4. He dies in the Lord, by whom eternal life is given.

These paintings were cleaned and restored by Professor Tristram in 1932, the cost being borne by the Friends of St. George's.

All the eight chapels in St. George's are of historic interest, and they are all legal ; for the law which, after the Reformation, prohibited the use of chantry chapels, excluded St. George's from its provisions. Chantry priests continued to be appointed down to the reign of King James I, but in his reign this was discontinued and the revenues were used for other purposes. Still to this day the wish and intention of the donors of these chapels are being carried out, for past benefactors are commemorated at special services held regularly during the year, and at the daily services the departed as well as the living are remembered in the prayer :—

" God save our Gracious Sovereign and all the Companions living and departed of the Most Noble Order of the Garter."

CHAPTER V

THE ROMANCE OF THE TOMBS AND MEMORIALS

KING EDWARD IV

I N his will King Edward IV left careful instructions regarding his tomb, which had been put in hand during his lifetime. It lies to the north of the high altar on the Yorkist side of the chapel. The tomb was covered with touch-stone or black marble on which stood the gates which John Tresilian had made for the purpose; trophies of honour overlaid with pearls, rubies and gold hung secure over the tomb until the chapel was plundered during the Commonwealth.

Early in 1789, while the paving in the north choir aisle was being repaired, an opening into the vault was disclosed, within which were found the coffins of King Edward IV and Queen Elizabeth Widville, his wife. The public flocked to the site and many of them found ways and means of gratifying their curiosity. This was soon stopped and the vault sealed up. The black marble slab on the wall at the back of the tomb, with the name Edward IIII in letters of solid brass, was then placed there, together with the brass lettering on the black touch-stone over the vault.

KING HENRY VI

In telling the story of the various chapels within St. George's we had cause to draw attention to the brutality of King Richard III. There is one thing for which he must thankfully be remembered. He was responsible for the removal of the earthly remains of King Henry VI from Chertsey to Windsor. In August 1484, the King's body was taken out of his grave in the church of Chertsey, where it had been buried by the orders of King Edward IV, and it was re-buried with all honour on the Lancastrian side of the chapel on the south of the high altar.

On 4th November, 1910, the tomb was opened and an investigation made, in the presence of representatives of the Chapter and Eton College (of which he was the founder), and a few other privileged persons. The leaden chest contained the bones of one whose size corresponded with that of King Henry VI, and the evidence that his body was brought from Chertsey and buried on the south side of the altar is conclusive.

Year by year on founder's day, the vice-provost, with a few representative boys from Eton college, lays a bunch of lilies on this tomb, where lies the body of a king to whom "learning was more glorious than royalty and books more precious than a crown."[1] The remains of an inscription on the south wall opposite the tomb bear evidence to the fact that the tomb was once much more glorious than it is to-day. The marble

[1] *Romance of Canterbury Cathedral*, page 74.

CHOIR STALL SHOWING GARTER PLATES

stone over the vault was placed there in 1790. For many years the beautiful pilgrims' money box, which was made by John Tresilian, stood near by ; it now stands at the south door of the nave.

The royal motto " Dieu et mon Droit " is connected with King Henry VI in the following way. It was first used by King Richard I as a pass-word or battle-cry before the battle of Gisors in France. He wished to emphasize the fact that he was not a vassal of France but a King by the grace of God in his own right. It was used by King Edward III when he claimed the crown of France through his mother, a French princess, and it became the permanent royal motto when King Henry VI was crowned King of France in Paris.

KING HENRY VIII

There can be no doubt that King Henry VIII intended to utilise for his own memorial all the costly material that Cardinal Wolsey had prepared for his own tomb within the chapel to the east of St. George's, now the Prince Consort Memorial Chapel. This chapel was appropriated by King Henry VIII when Wolsey fell from power, and so it passed from the control of the Chapter and became the property of the Crown. Large sums of money were spent by the King in converting the magnificent tomb of Wolsey into a memorial to himself. The work was never completed, and many of the costly fittings, including four huge bronze candlesticks, were sold during the Commonwealth period.

These candlesticks are now in the cathedral of St.

Bavon in Ghent; the two at present in the chapel are copies, and were given by King George and Queen Mary in memory of their four parents who were married before this altar and interred in the vaults below.

The will of King Henry VIII directed "that our body be buried and interred in the quire of our College of Windsor, midway between the stalls and the high Altar, with the body of my true and loving Queen Jane and there be made and set as soon as conveniently may be done after our disease by our executor, at our cost and charges, if it be not done by us in our life time, an honourable tomb for our bones to rest in. . . ."

The instructions contained in this will were carried out, and the tomb must have borne some inscription, but what it was we do not know. At the time of the burial of King Charles I the tomb was not marked, for it was only after a considerable search had been made that the vault containing the coffins of King Henry VIII and Queen Jane Seymour was found.

The ceremony of the burial of King Henry VIII was carried out in great pomp, and an account given of the closing scene runs as follows : " 16 strong Yeomen of the Guard took the coffin and with four strong linen towels, which they had for their fees, let it into the vault near unto the body of Queen Jane Seymour, his third wife. Then the Lord Chamberlain, the Lord Great Master, Mr. Treasurer, Mr. Comptroller and the Sergeant Porter, breaking their white staves upon their heads in three parts, as did likewise all the Gentlemen Ushers, threw them into the grave. Thus the funeral ended, the trumpets sounded in the Rood loft and the company dispersed."

KING CHARLES I

The snow is falling fast, the difficulty of finding a resting place for the body of the King has been solved. One of the Military Knights, secretly and like Nicodemus by night, has told of a vault in the choir said to contain the bodies of King Henry VIII and Jane Seymour: this has been found, and now with solemn tread a sad procession files into the chapel through the west doors. The coffin covered with velvet has rested for the night in the deanery; it is now covered with snow as it enters the building. The Duke of Richmond, Marquis of Hertford, Lord Southampton, Lord Lindsey and Herbert Mildmay form part of the procession. Cromwellian soldiers stand about the doors. A few remove their hats, the rest look on and stare.

Silently the procession passes through the nave into the choir, Bishop Juxon, who was with the King at the end, leading the way. The choir and indeed the whole of the chapel is much disfigured, and much that has been thoughtlessly broken is lying about in confusion, the ornaments from the altar have been removed and for the time being the glory has departed. The Governor of the Castle stands grimly looking on. The orders from the Council of State are to be carefully carried out. The Bishop may not use the prayer-book service, for the prayer-book has been proscribed. All that can be done is to lower the coffin white with snow into the vault, and in silence to lay the body of their King and their friend beside the coffins of King Henry VIII and his

Queen, and to commend his soul to the care of the King of kings. The ceremony is soon over, the little party disperses; King Charles has died, but King Charles in the person of his son shall, so they vow together, live and reign.

A hundred and fifty-four years pass by. Around the tomb there stands, reverent, another group of men. It has been said that the body of King Charles I was not laid to rest in the choir of St. George's, and now the truth is to be known. Carefully the vault is uncovered, reverently the lead coffin is opened, the truth is established. It contains without doubt the body of King Charles I, for the likeness is recognised before the body crumbles to dust.

Yet once again the scene is changed, though the setting still remains the same. A small group surrounds the tomb one evening in 1888, the vault is opened, and into it there is passed a small casket containing a few fragments of the body of the murdered King, which had been removed when the vault was opened in 1813. In the centre of the group stands Albert Edward, Prince of Wales, anxious that these precious relics shall be restored to the tomb. The sun has gone down, twilight is turning into darkness, and the vault once more is sealed.

Additional evidence to the fact that this vault contains the bodies of Queen Jane Seymour, King Henry VIII, King Charles I and an infant child of Queen Anne (as is recorded on the marble slab placed there in the reign of King William IV), is to be found in a manuscript memorandum written by Mr. Sewell, for forty years

Chapter Clerk. He stated that upon opening this vault for the interment of a stillborn child of the Princess of Denmark, afterwards Queen Anne, he went into the vault and there saw the coffins of King Henry VIII and Queen Jane, also the coffin of King Charles I covered with velvet with a label on the cover, whereon was marked " King Charles 1648."[1] The vault was small and the new-born child was laid upon the coffin of King Charles I.

CHAPTER VI

The Romance of the Tombs and Memorials (Continued)

THE ROYAL VAULT

KING GEORGE III, to whose care and generosity St. George's owes much, caused a large vault to be made which runs under the altar and under the Prince Consort Memorial Chapel. In this vault lie the bodies of King George III, King George IV, King William IV and many other members of the royal family. The bodies of Queen Victoria and Prince Albert rest in the private mausoleum erected by Queen Victoria in the gardens of Frogmore House in the home park; while those of King Edward VII and his Consort lie under their effigies in the chapel.

It will be noticed that in St. George's Chapel are buried sovereigns of each dynasty since the time of King

[1] i.e., 1648-9, the execution being on Jan. 30 and the beginning of a year at this period being dated from March 25.

F

Edward III :—King Henry VI (Lancaster), King Edward IV (York), King Henry VIII (Tudor), King Charles I (Stuart), King George III and his successors of the house of Hanover.

CHARLES BRANDON

The chapel is filled with tombs and memorials of great interest. It is impossible within the limits of this book to call attention to them all or to mention more than a few of the inscriptions which record faithful service in all parts of the world.

In the south choir aisle is the tomb of Charles Brandon, Duke of Suffolk. He married King Henry VIII's sister, who had been Queen of France. He distinguished himself at the siege of Tournay and was the hero of many tournaments. His courage and humility, his generosity and handsome presence won for him universal esteem. He was the first English subject to be admitted to that great Order of France, the Order of St. Michael, and after him only two other Englishmen were admitted.

At a tournament in France the French were so envious at his successes that they introduced a gigantic German in the hope that he would defeat the British hero. Charles Brandon, however, caught him by the neck and beat him so violently with the pommel of his sword that the French interfered and carried away their hoped-for champion.

JACOBI FIELD

Another tomb of interest is that of Jacobi Field in the north choir aisle. He was commissary for the Church overseas. In the Chapter Library there is a small Testament translated into Iroquois and printed at Cambridge, Massachusetts, in 1665 ; it is possible that this book was sent to Dr. Field because of his active interest in and his official connection with the work of the Church overseas. He died in 1727.

JEFFRY WYATVILLE

In the ambulatory at the east end is the tomb of Sir Jeffry Wyatville (1766–1840). His arms incorporate the George IV gateway, in the Castle, and part of his crest is the Round Tower. During the reigns of King George IV, King William IV and Queen Victoria all the work done at the Castle by way of new construction and restoration was carried out under his direction.

CANON DALTON

The last interment was that of John Neale Dalton in 1931. He was tutor to His Majesty King George V for thirteen years, and Canon of Windsor for forty-six years. His dramatic reading of the lessons will long be remembered, and his devoted work during the restoration of the chapel is mentioned in another chapter.

BAPTIST MAY

His tomb is in the Rutland Chapel ; he was keeper of the privy purse to King Charles II, and took a keen interest in the work which Wren carried out at Windsor Castle.

He was responsible for bringing Grinling Gibbons to the notice of the king, and died in 1696.

Outside the vestry door there is a memorial to Weetman Dickinson Pearson, first Viscount Cowdray, who died 1927. On it is recorded the fact that he was " a great lover of this noble Chapel which he helped to preserve."

A marble bust of Lieut.-General Sir John Elley tells of one who entering the army as a private raised himself to the rank of lieut.-general. He served with distinction all through the Peninsular war, was wounded at Waterloo and became M.P. for Windsor in 1835. Opposite this memorial is one to John Mitchell who for no less than seventy-six years was a member of the choir.

On a brass beneath the organ loft George Brooke, Yeoman of the Guard in the reigns of King Henry VIII, King Edward VI, Queen Mary and Queen Elizabeth, is commemorated in the following quaint lines :

> " He lyved content with meane estat
> and long ago prepared to dye
> The idle parson he did hate
> poore peoples want he did supply."

On the floor of the ambulatory, near the stairway to the song-room is the tombstone of David Stokes, a Canon and notable scholar, who died in 1669. The writer of the Latin epitaph, having mentioned that Stokes was skilled in " Latin, Greek, Hebrew, Chaldaic, Arabic and Syriac," adds (in verse) that one who in a few years studied

> " so many languages, and mastered each,
> now will learn easily the angelic speech."

The Naval Knights of Windsor, who used to live in what is now St. George's choir school, are commemorated on a curious brass plate which has on it a picture of a ship and the words " Ye heavenward bound Ship." The memorial was erected to Lieutenant Charles Okes, R.N., " for 30 years one of Ye Naval Knights of which Society he died as Governor " in 1860.

Outside Dean Urswick's Chapel there is a memorial brass erected by Queen Victoria to the son of the Emperor of Abyssinia whose name, Alamaya, means " I have seen the World." Lord Napier, after the taking of Magdala in Abyssinia, in 1868, brought the Prince back to England. Queen Victoria took him under her care and sent him to Eton, but he died in 1879 and was buried outside the west end of the chapel.

Among several memorials to Military Knights of Windsor one should be mentioned, that of Colonel Francis Cornwallis Maude, V.C. He had a most distinguished career and died in 1900. The memorial was erected by friends in the order of Military Knights and by his surviving comrades who held him in high esteem.

The bravery of a soldier on the field of battle is recorded in a memorial to Robert Christopher Packe, Royal Horse Guards, Blue, who was killed at the head of his squadron at the battle of Waterloo, and whose brother officers erected the memorial.

Mention must also be made of a memorial to Sir Henry Frederick Ponsonby for twenty-five years Private Secretary to Queen Victoria, and his wife, Mary Elizabeth, Maid of Honour to the Queen. For thirty-four years they resided within the precincts of Windsor Castle. Also of Lord Gerald Wellesley, nephew of the Iron Duke, who was for thirty-three years Domestic Chaplain to Queen Victoria and for twenty-eight years Dean of Windsor.

THE DUKE OF KENT

We must close this short list of selected memorials and tombs with just two more. One is the effigy of the Duke of Kent, the father of Queen Victoria, executed by the famous sculptor Boehm.

MARY DUCHESS OF GLOUCESTER

The other is that erected by Queen Victoria to the memory of her aunt, Mary, Duchess of Gloucester, daughter of King George III. The work was designed by Gilbert Scott, and the panels above the tombs are representations in marble of St. Matthew XXV. vv. 35, 36, " Naked and ye clothed me. I was an hungred and ye gave me meat. I was a stranger and ye took me in. I was sick and ye visited me." Such a one was Mary Duchess of Gloucester to all who were in distress.

If we had space there are many more stories that could be told of those whose names are commemorated within these walls and in the cloisters, but perhaps enough has been told to show how in its tombs and memorials St. George's is full of romance.

SOUTH-WEST CORNER OF CHOIR
Sovereign's Stall

CHAPTER VII

THE ROMANCE OF THE GARTER PLATES

IT is not generally realised that St. George's Chapel contains, next to Westminster Abbey, probably more examples of first-rate craftsmanship than any other church in England; and of all its treasures none are more precious than the stall plates of the Knights of the Garter. The oldest of these are unique examples of enamel on gilt or silvered copper, and were brought into St. George's from the previous chapel of the Order, during the reign of King Richard III. Down to the 17th century they were enamelled, from then until 1908 the coats of arms were usually painted on the copper; after that date enamel once more was used.

If all the plates were in existence there should be 812; but some were never erected, others have been removed when Knights were degraded, and others have been either lost or stolen. One of those removed on the degradation of a Knight in 1553, is now in the British Museum; and another which was stolen was found in a marine store in New Zealand in 1898. This plate is that of Charles Somerset, Earl of Worcester, 1514. It has now been restored to its original position. Nearly 600 plates are now in the chapel, and in that number there are no fewer than ninety varieties. Students of heraldry can find here a fruitful ground for their studies, and others can see in them in miniature the history of the Knights of the Garter from 1367 down to the present day.

The installation of a Knight is too elaborate a ceremony to be described in this book, but space must be found to give the wording of the Admonition and the Oath. The Knight is admonished to be " not only strong to fight but also to offer himself to shed his blood, for Christ's Faith, the liberties of the Church and the just and necessary defence of the oppressed and needy." The oath taken runs as follows :

" You being chosen to be one of the honourable Company of this most noble Order of the Garter, shall promise and swear by the Holy Evangelists, by you here touched, that wittingly and willingly you shall not break any Statute of the said Order, or any Articles in them contained, the same being agreeable and not repugnant to the Laws of Almighty God and the laws of this realm, as far forth as to you belongeth and appertaineth. So help you God and his holy Word."

When a Knight was degraded, the following procedure was followed. The Garter King at Arms stood on the highest of the steps leading up to the brass lectern, which was originally the Chanter's desk and dates from early in the 16th century; the Officers at Arms stood around him, the Black Rod also being present, while he read aloud the notice of the Knight's degradation. This being done, one of the Heralds being placed on the back of the Knight's stall took his crest and violently cast it down into the choir, and afterwards his banner and sword; all the Officers of Arms then spurned these emblems out of the choir into the body of the chapel and then out of the west door, thence through the Castle gate and into the river. Such a grim proceeding has not often taken place in the history of this great order of chivalry, nor has such a severe sentence been always deserved. It is a happier theme to dwell on all the noble deeds done by the Knights of the Garter since the foundation of the order; and as we have on another page a picture of the Garter plates at the back of one stall, let us briefly tell the story that four of these plates commemorate.

At the top of our picture are the arms of Ralph Lord Basset. This is the oldest plate in the chapel and dates from the middle of the 14th century. Lord Basset took an honourable part in the wars in the Holy Land and in Spain; and under the leadership of the Black Prince, son of King Edward III, he distinguished himself at the battle of Poitiers. It was this victory and others won in France and Scotland that caused King Edward III to be shown in pictures as having on his sword the crowns of France and Scotland.

Another plate on the picture is that of Sir William FitzWilliam, Earl of Southampton. In 1513 he was one of the chief commanders in the fleet and " was sore hurt with a quarrel " against the French off Brest. He held many high offices as Admiral and General, and after surviving a severe attack of " sweating sickness," he died leading the army into Scotland. In such esteem was he held that after his death his standard was borne throughout the whole campaign. " He was keen, bold and

G

sagacious, and being able to resist flattery he never lost his presence of mind."

Another of these plates is that of the Earl of Huntingdon who was Lieut. General and Chief Captain of the Army and Fleet for service abroad in 1549. He not only complained of the ill-equipment of his troops during service in France, but did his best to see that those serving under him were properly fed and looked after. He declared for Lady Jane Grey, and was taken to the Tower in 1553, but was released six months later. It is to his credit that he strenuously opposed the revival of the old penalty against heresy. He died in 1561.

Coming to more modern times, our picture includes the plate of the 2nd Earl Spencer. From 1794–1801 he was first Lord of the Admiralty, being held in general esteem by the navy. While he was at the Admiralty Nelson won some of his greatest victories at sea, and retrieved the fortunes of the country, which had been greatly endangered by the ill-success of the army on land.

Such is the story that lies behind these Garter plates, the story of men who, for the most part, added lustre to their country's annals in their several generations. This brief sketch of a few of the Knights of the Garter, taken almost haphazard from the back of one stall, gives point to the prayer that is offered daily for " all the Companions, living and departed, of the most noble Order of the Garter." The plates are at present very crowded in some of the stalls, and a rearrangement is being considered.

SOUTH-WEST CORNER OF CHOIR
Sovereign's Stall

CHAPTER VIII

THE ROMANCE OF THE CARVING

THE carved and canopied stalls of the choir were
begun in 1478 and finished and fixed in their places
by 1485. They are of great beauty and are said
to be the only set of stalls in England of which there
is a detailed account. William Berkeley was the head
carver, and the Chapter accounts give the names of other
carvers together with the amounts paid to them for their
work.

Originally there were fifty stalls, namely four return
stalls on each side of the entrance to the choir and twenty-
one along the north and south sides. The return stalls were
for the Knights of the Royal Family, that of the King
and the Prince of Wales being placed next to the
entrance, on the south and north sides respectively.

The twenty-one stalls on each side were arranged
alternately for the Knights and Canons, those for
the Knights having a high canopy surmounted with
crest, helmet mantling and sword. When the number
of foreign Honorary Knights was increased the Canons
were deprived of their stalls, and the whole row of
high canopies with their regalia and banners must have
produced a somewhat crowded effect. This has now to
some extent been remedied, for there has been a large
reduction in the number of foreign Knights, and an

addition has been made to the number of the stalls, of which mention will be made later.

Along the desk fronts of the stalls were carved in beautiful lettering the words of the 20th Psalm and a verse from the 84th Psalm, and on the backs of the lowest row of stalls there are carvings of a varied assortment of subjects. No detailed account can be given in this chapter of the exquisite design of the panels which join the stalls on the north and south sides with the return stalls; this was all part of the original work. A full description of this beautiful carving, together with the subjects carved on all the desk fronts and the 'popeys' or desk ends, has been given by Dr. M. R. James, O.M., Provost of Eton, in *The Woodwork of the Choir*.

Some mention must be made of the misericords; in these grotesque carvings the craftsman apparently did not work to a design, but followed his own fancy, and we can see in his work a reflection of the spirit and thought of his time. Thus two misericords, both on the south side, illustrate the same idea: on one there is a fox in a gown and hood standing in a pulpit and preaching to two geese, a goose in his hood and another in his hand; on the other misericord three monks and a fox are being trundled along in a wheel-barrow by Satan into the open jaws of hell. When we remember that a fox in those days was the usual representation of a friar we get from these carvings some idea of the mistrust of monks and friars which had already begun to make itself felt before the Reformation in England took place. These monks and friars had done a great work in the country, but eagerness for power and wealth had led to a lessening of their spiritual influence.

During the Commonwealth considerable damage was done to the woodwork in the chapel, but after the Restoration much was done to repair the damage and to replace what had been taken away; Wren however was unable to accomplish all that he wished owing to lack of funds. To King Charles II and to other members of the Royal Family we owe the handsome silver gilt candlesticks and the altar vessels given to replace all the valuable gold plate that Cromwell had taken and sold. Just enough was left for actual use, which shows that Communion services were held in St. George's during the Commonwealth. These vessels are still in use, among them a Marian alms-dish of considerable value.

It was not until the reign of King George III that all the woodwork was properly repaired. Emlyn was called in to carry out the work of restoration and alteration; he was a wood carver before he became an architect, and for this St. George's may indeed be thankful. The damaged canopies and carvings were dealt with by him with such skill that there is difficulty in distinguishing Emlyn's work from the original. He was equally successful in his additions to the woodwork, for it was he who carved the case for the organ, and the beauty of his work can still be seen, although at the last restoration much of it had to be altered and refitted. The two additional stalls at the east end on either side of the choir were a masterpiece of imitation, indeed it would be difficult to detect this addition were it not for the altered lettering on the desk front of these stalls; Psalm 20 was broken into and on the sovereign's side there are the words " God save the King," while on the Prince of Wales' side are the words " God bless the Prince."

On the desk fronts of the second row of these stalls Emlyn introduced incidents in the life of King George III. On the south side we see the attempted murder of the King by Margaret Nicholson; six little girls walking two and two and a seventh before a lady in a large hat, the scene laid in an avenue in the park of Windsor Castle; and others represent Royalty visiting the Foundling Hospital. On the north side King George III and his Queen are shown at St. Paul's Cathedral, where a great service of thanksgiving was held on 23rd April, 1789.

To Emlyn we also owe all the doors which give access to the stalls, and he added the beautiful tester which lends dignity to the Sovereign's stall. All this work was carried out with exquisite skill, and preserves to an extraordinary degree the character of the old work, as can be seen from the picture of the south-west corner of the choir; in this illustration we see how beautifully the tester over the Sovereign's stall harmonizes with the original carved work around it. The other illustration of the woodwork carries us back to the earliest days of our story; it is a panel on a desk front on the north side of the choir. The shield and badge within the Garter is that of Bishop Beauchamp; the snails which form his badge may be seen in the stonework in other parts of the chapel; his arms are a fess between six martlets, which have been cut away, and on the border of the shield are eight bells or doctors' caps.

CHOIR DESK, BISHOP BEAUCHAMP'S ARMS

In the chapel there are several chairs and benches of great interest; the doors and screens reveal the beauty of their craftsmanship, some belonging to the same period as the choir stalls, others of a later date, as for instance the south doors of the nave; these can be dated by the nail heads being in the form of the hemp-brake of Sir Reginald Braye which he introduced very freely into all the work done under his supervision.

The woodwork in St. George's is a product of English craftsmanship of the last quarter of the 15th century, supplemented by work done under the Tudor dynasty and during the last part of the 18th century. Many happy hours can be spent in tracing out the stories and the imagery which are so wonderfully portrayed in all this exquisite carving and which the Provost of Eton describes as being unrivalled in this country for richness and delicacy.

CHAPTER IX

THE ROMANCE OF THE MUSIC

IT is not possible to describe with any accuracy the design of the original rood-loft between the choir and the nave, or to say what it contained: but we may with safety conclude that towards the end of King Edward IV's reign it contained a desk from which the Gospels were sung and some kind of organ, or organs as they were then called.

From the foundation of the Order of the Garter, music had an all-important place in the rules laid down by King Edward III, but it is not until the reign of King Henry VIII that any connected story can be told. During the latter part of this reign John Marbecke was organist. The choir of St. George's apparently took an active part in the Reformation controversies, for Marbecke and two other Lay Clerks were condemned to death at the stake in 1544. Marbecke was pardoned through the intervention of Bishop Gardiner; but the two others were burnt in what is now the Chapter Garden.

In 1550 Marbecke published a musical work entitled " The boke of Common Praier noted," and being a theologian as well as a musician he brought out the first Concordance of the English Bible. In the course of a long dedication of this Concordance to King Edward VI he describes himself as " destitute bothe of learnying and eloquence, yea, and suche a one as in maner never tasted the swetness of learned Letters, but altogether brought up in your highnes College at Wyndesore, in the study of Musike and plaiying on Organs wherein I consumed vainly the greatest part of my life."

In " Tudor Church Music " published for the Carnegie Trust by the Oxford University Press, the following quotation from Marbecke's Concordance occurs. " This worke hath escaped so many jeoperdies and nowe finished and brought to light . . . as I had almoste finished the same, my chaunce among others was, at Windsore to bee taken in a labirinth, and troublesome net of a law called the Statute of VI Articles, where, by meanes of good workers for my dispatch, I was quickly condempned and judged to death, for the copiying out of a worke, made by the greate Clerke Master, Jhon Calvin, written against the same sixe articles. . . . But the livying lorde, who brought Daniell out of the lake of Lions and sent the Prophete Abacuck to beare hym foode, moved the haste of the noble and famous Prince, your highnes father to graunte me his most gracious pardon, whiche I enjoyed and was set at libertie."

Through the influence of a friend he expected the support of King Henry VIII for publishing the Concordance, as well as that of " The Quene, your highnes fathers most verteous and Godly last wife " ; but " before the quenes grace could hav tyme convenient, to move the Kynges highness, God tooke hym to his mercie and anone I lost her grace also. . . . And then I was utterly in despaire, that it should ever forward. But when I sawe that God has set your moste excellent Majestie in this Royall seate, I was anone as a man newly revived in spirit : . . . I yet once again a newe writte out the same, in suche sorte as the worke now appereth, and by the providence of God is now finished." This was no mean task, for the Concordance in its final form contained several hundred pages, each of which was divided into three columns.

During the reign of King Edward VI, under the protectorate of the Duke of Somerset, organ playing was banned; for the Injunctions of King Edward VI to the Chapter dated 26th October, 1550, stated as follows, " And whereas we understand that John Marbecke and George Thaxton, hath of your graunt, ffees appointed them severally for playing upon organs. We take ordre

H

that the sayd John and George shall enjoy their severall ffees during their lyves, if they continue in that Colledge, in as large and ample maner as if organ plaing had still continued in the Churche."

John Marbecke died about 1585. Other notable organists and choir masters during the Tudor period who were attached to St. George's were Richard Farrant, John Mundy and Nathaniel Giles. During Mundy's term of office Thomas Dallam, organ builder, set over the choir door an organ enlarged and rebuilt from the existing organ or organs already in the chapel.

During the Commonwealth the choir was disbanded; but at the Restoration, Dr. Child, who was organist in 1632, returned to his former position and lived to the age of ninety. He was mentioned frequently by Samuel Pepys in his diary; and Dr. Fellowes, in his chapter on the music of St. George's Chapel, published in " Windsor Castle, St. George's Chapel and Choir," tells of him the following story. " For many years in the reign of Charles II Child's salary as one of the organists of the Chapel Royal remained unpaid, and the arrears amounted to as much as £500. Regarding it as a bad debt, and discussing the subject one day with some of the Canons of Windsor, he declared himself ready to sell the debt to anyone for £5 and a few bottles of wine. The challenge was accepted by the Canons, and the price was paid.

" Some years later James II discharged many of his brother's debts, including this one, and Child loudly lamented the bad bargain he had concluded. But the Canons came forward with a most generous proposal and consented to release Child of his bargain, on condi-

THE ORGAN, LOOKING EAST

tion that he would pay for the paving of the choir. To this he agreed; and no doubt a fair sum was left over as a residue. The fact that he paved the choir, as it is to-day, is recorded on his tombstone near the entrance to the organ gallery."

The present gallery was built during the reign of King George III. It is made of Coade's artificial stone from the designs of Emlyn. A new organ built by Green was given by the King. The excellence of this instrument will be recognised when it is known that though additions were made to it in 1835, and the organ rebuilt and brought up to date in 1883, and again in 1930, a number of the pipes belonging to Green's organ are still in use.

Sir George Elvey became organist in 1835; and on his retirement in 1882, he was succeeded by Sir Walter Parratt, who held the post with much distinction until his death in 1924. Sir Walford Davies was invited to succeed him, but was unable to do so until 1927. During the interim, Dr. Fellowes, whose knowledge of Tudor music is unrivalled, directed the choir, the organ being played by Mr. Malcolm Boyle, now organist of Chester Cathedral.

In 1930 the organ was entirely rebuilt and divided into two main parts so as to give an uninterrupted view of the whole of the vaulted roof. The work was carried out by J. W. Walker & Sons and Rothwell & Son, in consultation with Sir Walford Davies. A great innovation was made by the introduction of two keyboards, which opens the way for fresh development in organ playing. Sir Walford Davies' retirement in 1932 was soon followed by the sad death of Mr. Hylton Stewart, and in 1933 Dr. Harris, from Christ Church Cathedral, Oxford, became organist.

Experts say that there is no building more perfect for sound than St. George's; and organists from all parts of the world come to see and to hear how beautifully the services, on weekdays as well as on Sundays, can be rendered.

This chapter must not close without a reference to " Spur Money " which in the past has brought much joy to the hearts of the boys in the choir. " Spur Money is the fine paid for the redemption of the spurs worn by any person within the Royal Free Chapel of St. George at Windsor, which spurs are otherwise forfeit to the choristers of the same. This fine has been paid from time immemorial up to the present day." In the old days 6s. 8d. was demanded ; the equivalent in modern money would be several pounds.

King Henry VII and King Henry VIII both paid the fine, the latter on several occasions. In recent years the colonel of a regiment objected to the fine, but his objection was not upheld. Let every chorister keep his eyes open, for the possibility of pocket money may at any time occur ; but let him see that he can repeat his gamut (the musical scale) or else the wearer of spurs, who demands that this be done, will pass out of the chapel with the contents of his pockets intact.

St. George's Chapel is a great national inheritance ; services and festivals of music are frequently held in the nave which give emphasis to its national character. The intention of such services and festivals is to reinforce and not to replace the position held by parish churches.

At the ordinary services, held in the choir, the public are most welcome; but it must be remembered that the seating accommodation is small. What is hoped is that all who come will feel that the services are in keeping with the restful beauty of the building, and will go away uplifted and refreshed.

CHAPTER X

THE ROMANCE OF THE WINDOWS

A GREAT deal of the romance of St. George's is contained in the stained glass of its windows. How much of the glass was destroyed during the Commonwealth we do not know. What we do know is that practically all the 15th century glass now to be seen in the chapel was collected by Dr. Lockman in 1774 and placed together in the west window. A few other pieces of old glass survive in the chapel of Dr. Oliver King and in the clerestory windows in the nave.

Some twenty years later, Benjamin West drew up a design for a new west window similar to the east window which he had already put in. This design was highly approved by King George III, and a considerable portion of the window was finished. We may indeed be thankful that it was never erected, but left in the factory where it was made. The east window only survived sixty years before it was removed. Benjamin West's work as a designer of stained glass windows was not destined to live in St. George's.

Tastes differ from age to age, but we may hope that never again will it be thought right to replace 15th century glass by that of a later date. We may indeed be thankful that the glorious west window survived, and at the last restoration (1920-1930) with the help of Dr. M. R. James, all the figures in this most beautiful window were put into a definite order. They represent warrior saints, archbishops and bishops of many centuries. The glass in the upper part of the window and the inscription at the bottom were the work of Willement in 1848. He was the first man in modern times to realise the right use of heraldry in windows.

There is history to be learnt from the four crowns that appear in these windows. That of King Edward tells of the founder of the Order of the Garter. The crown of King Edward IV speaks of the first builder of the chapel. Below that of King Henry VII is the hawthorn tree of Bosworth field, while that of Queen Elizabeth of York tells how the warring houses of York and Lancaster were united by her marriage with King Henry VII, on which occasion it is said a bouquet of white and red roses was carried by the Queen.

The clerestory windows in the choir and the nave tell their own story, for they contain the arms of the Knights of the Garter from the reign of King George III down to the latter part of Queen Victoria's reign. The painted glass in the windows of the north and south aisles of the choir is the work of Willement about the middle of the 19th century. In the windows a succession of royal personages is portrayed, and there is some beautiful heraldic glass.

NAVE, LOOKING WEST

The east window, by Clayton and Bell, was put in when Sir Gilbert Scott restored the stone tracery to its original beauty, the marble and alabaster reredos being also his work. The window and reredos were given by the Dean and Canons in memory of the Prince Consort. In the window, centred around the incarnate and risen Christ, are Biblical heroes whose example, it was felt, the Prince Consort had followed. At the top of the window Our Lord appears in glory with angels and archangels, while at the bottom are representative incidents in the public and private life of the Prince Consort, whose strict devotion to duty was the cause of his death while in the prime of life. The window was displayed for the first time on the occasion of the marriage of the Prince of Wales on March 10th, 1863, to the lovely Princess Alexandra of Denmark.

Beneath this window, to the south of the altar, lie the bodies of King Edward VII and Queen Alexandra, their recumbent marble effigies by Sir Bertram Mackennal. It is fitting that they should rest there, for in this royal chapel King Edward VII was baptised and married.

One other window should be mentioned, that over the north door in the nave. The figures in this window were suggested by the late Canon Dalton and the work executed by Clayton and Bell. It was given by the Old Boys of St. George's Choir School in memory of those from this school who gave their lives for God, King and Country during the Great War. Among the names recorded is that of Lieut. J. N. Bigge, the only son of Lord Stamfordham, to whose wisdom the country and empire owe much and to whose memory no adequate

tribute in words could be paid. Beneath the names is
the symbol of warfare happily accomplished, a sword
laid aside with a laurel wreath upon it, in the midst of
spring flowers, and a sunrise beyond the sea with a gleam
of light falling upon a cross, the symbol of new life
above the warrior's grave.

Though not a window, mention may here be made of
the fine tapestry which now hangs near the entrance to
the north choir-aisle. This was woven in King Charles I's
works at Mortlake, after one of his own pictures,
" Christ at Emmaus " by Titian. King Charles had bought
the picture from the Duke of Mantua; but Cromwell
sold it, and it is now in the Louvre. The arms on the
shield at the top are those of John, first Viscount Mordaunt,
who was Constable of Windsor Castle in 1660. His widow
presented it to the chapel, where it used to hang over
the altar until 1707. It has recently been skilfully
restored, and placed behind glass for its better preser-
vation—another of the benefits owed to the Friends of
St. George's.

The popularity of St. George's shows no signs of
diminishing. It is no uncommon thing for upwards of
5,000 to visit the chapel on Bank holidays. We may
indeed be thankful that the windows contain no glass to
mar the pleasure of the visitors; and anyone who under-
takes the pleasant task of showing people round the chapel
will find that his knowledge of history, heraldry, stained
glass, architecture and craftsmanship is not unduly over-
taxed, for the two most popular questions are: Where
was King Charles I buried, and where does the present
King sit when he comes here for services?

CHAPTER XI

THE ROMANCE OF THE LAST RESTORATION

SIR CHRISTOPHER WREN, whose father was Dean of Windsor, reported on the serious condition of St. George's and in 1682 strengthened the roof and other portions of the building. Indeed but for Wren's repairs to the roof it might long ago have been past mending.

During the 18th century though much was done to the inside of the chapel the fabric received little attention. In *The Times* of March 6th, 1928, appeared an article on the work of repairs in which the following passage occurs :

" The cracks and flaws which had begun to appear in warning of ultimate disaster had been tidily plastered over by a shocked 18th century, which did not wish to pay for the many repairs and did not like to be reminded either of the need or its neglect. So it applied tenpenny-worth of plaster and pretence instead of pounds' worth of stone and common sense and trusted to luck and posterity to make good King Henry VII's shortcomings and its own parsimonious procrastinations."

A careful survey of the whole chapel by Sir Harold Brakespear in 1918 revealed a state of things that could

I

brook no delay. The great tie-beams of oak, which had been given by Bishop Beauchamp when the chapel was built, were hardly long enough for their purpose and did not rest sufficiently on the walls, which were themselves unfinished. The decay of these beams and the ravages of the death-watch beetle, coupled with the condition of the masonry on which they rested, made them a danger instead of a support to the roof. The foundations in many parts of the chapel were found to be unsound and had given way, and the cracks in the roof were so alarming that there was grave danger of the vaulted roof falling in.

In 1920 the work of restoration was begun. The principle adhered to during the whole of the repairs was that no fresh material should be used where the old could be made to serve. The foundations were first made secure. Next it was found necessary to erect the noble buttresses which now add dignity to the exterior of the north and south transepts; there were no buttresses to the transepts before, and the roof was insufficiently supported. The buttresses to the nave and choir were always there, and the prodigious thrust and weight of the vaulted ceiling was communicated to them by the flying buttresses which contribute so much to the grace of the exterior. These essential flying buttresses had however become perilously eroded by the action of the weather; they were on the verge of collapse, and had to be renewed with fresh stone.

Inside the chapel a partition was erected from floor to ceiling across the head of the nave, and for seven years the services were held in the nave while the choir was attended to. The roof was dismantled bay by bay, each stone being taken down, examined, and eventually re-assembled with meticulous accuracy. The choir was reopened for services just before Easter in 1927. After an interval of nearly 300 years the King's Beasts which Wren had been obliged to remove appeared once more on the pinnacles of the choir and transepts ; when those had been removed Wren had advised the substitution of large stone pineapples for structural security, to give stability to the flying buttresses. This had not been done, but with the re-erection of the King's Beasts both what he desired was effected, and a genuine restoration was carried out. These heraldic monsters add beauty to the chapel, and can be seen from miles around.

During the next three years the work of restoration was carried out in the nave, the same care being taken to add new material only where necessity demanded. The pillars of the choir screen which support the organ were strengthened and the organ rebuilt as has been described in another chapter.

On the 4th of November, 1930, in brilliant sunshine, the re-opening of the completely restored chapel took place. The service was attended by King George V and Queen Mary, together with the members of the Royal Family. Sixteen Knights of the Garter were present, in addition to King Manoel, the Ambassadors of Italy, Spain, Belgium and Japan, and the Ministers of Sweden, Norway and Denmark who represented the foreign Royal members of the Order. Among others present were the Archbishop of Canterbury, the Prime Minister, the Lord Chancellor and the high officers of State. A service of great dignity and joyfulness followed, and among those whose hearts were filled with thoughts of deep thankfulness two in particular should be mentioned— the Dean, Dr. Baillie, on whom the whole burden of the financial responsibility had rested for ten long years, and Canon Dalton, to whose untiring energy and profound antiquarian learning the restored chapel owed so much.

The total cost of the restoration was £175,000. King George V, supported by the Knights of the Garter, was the first to help, but as the work progressed it was seen that the amount required was far in excess of what was at first anticipated. For some considerable time there was real anxiety as to whether sufficient money could be raised. It was during this period that the Dean received most valuable help from Mr. Sydney Walton in working out various means for raising funds ; timely aid was given also by the great building contractor, Mr. Minter, who was always ready to supply money at critical moments. His donations amounted in all to a large sum ; and he also defrayed the whole cost of the re-erection of the King's Beasts, which were carved in his workshop at Putney. The strain for a time was relieved by a very large donation from the late Lord Cowdray, and the restoration of the choir roof will be always associated with his name. Then, as still more money was needed, Lord Woolavington once more saved the situation with a magnificent gift which made it possible for the work of restoration in the nave to be accomplished. It must not be forgotten that, as well as these gifts, donations large and small, many anonymous, were sent from all the world over. Such was the interest aroused when it was known that St. George's Chapel was in danger.

Well indeed may Sir Harold Brakespear be proud of his work. Thanks to his skill as an architect, he was able to report that the chapel was now in a far more perfect and secure condition than it had ever been in its history. Mention must also be made of the builders, Messrs. John Thompson & Sons of Peterborough, of Mr. William Hopkins their foreman, Mr. R. B. Robertson the Chapter Surveyor and Clerk of the Works, and all the workmen employed. A task of such magnitude, requiring at every turn highly skilled craftsmen, reflects the greatest credit on everyone who during those ten years worked on the building. There is additional satisfaction in recording the fact that the work was carried out without any serious accident.

And so St. George's stands to-day, as of old, a thing of beauty. The mellowing touch of time will soon lessen the whiteness of the stones, inside and out ; and the tints of the repainted bosses on the roof and in some of the chapels will ere long cease to have the appearance of newly-finished work.

In a leading article of *The Times*, November 4th, 1930, it was written, " Perhaps nothing better could be wished for our land than that this material restoration should be quickly followed by a spiritual restoration of the ideals which such a place as St. George's seems to affirm—the English temper of self-discipline and restraint, the spirit of unrestrained chivalry and of individual effort for the common weal, the courage which in the face of omens however dismal will send us into battle with stout hearts, to fight our dragons and, please God, to slay them."

Let us end our romance with some lines written by Mrs. Everett, the wife of a devoted Minor Canon who worked in the chapel for thirty years and was the first secretary of the Friends of St. George's.

Spirit of man hath fashion'd it, and hand of man,
This matchless shrine, to one clean Vision dedicate;
Whence from its topmost walls symbolic devils flee,
And rows of angels comely and sedate, there gravely smile.
Spirit of man awake! Bar out the devils all!
Let it not plead in vain, this prayer in stone.
And as the ages roll, and as the Vision grows,
Behold its radiance pierces every dingy nook
In home and heart. And thus you triumph gloriously
Spirit of man who fashion'd it, and his who liveth it.

EPILOGUE

SINCE Canon Blackburne wrote this book another
association has been added to the Chapel. Another
King has been buried here. A King who will
always be remembered for his great and noble influence
during one of the most difficult periods of English history. Almost all the Kings who have been buried here
have had some special interest in the story of our country.
There was Henry VI, one of the greatest founders of
English education, and a man who for many generations
drew pilgrims to his grave by the saintliness of his life.
There was Henry VIII, who, though we may not admire
his character, ruled England with great wisdom and gave
it an established place among the nations of Europe.
There was Charles I, round whose memory so many
romantic associations cling. There was George III, whose
homely virtues won the love of his people, and who
loved the Chapel with a special love. There were Queen
Victoria and King Edward, who re-built the idea of
sovereignty on a new foundation. And now there is
George V, who built so nobly on those foundations.
They all speak of the great part that our Kings have
played in the life of the nation. And it is remarkable
how their influence in every case, except perhaps that
of Henry VIII, has come from their character. And that
is signally true in the case of the late King. He became

a great rock shadow in a weary land, a steadying influence in disturbed and difficult times because of his straight-
forward courageous character. There was one mark
about his funeral which was new. In the story of the
older funerals we read of black hangings and all the
sombre trappings of woe. This time, following his own
wishes, the funeral with all its solemnity was full of
the note of hope. There were no black hangings, and the
altar was draped in white, with white flowers and the
gleam of gold speaking of the hope of resurrection.
Never perhaps has there been a Royal funeral with more
genuine sorrow. But it was not the sorrow of men
without hope. We trust that his grave may be an inspiration to his subjects in facing the anxieties and troubles of
life.

NOTES ON THE ROYAL ARMS AND SOME HERALDIC TERMS

I T will be of interest to our readers if we describe some of the Royal Arms which can be seen in many parts of the chapel.

Heraldry is the symbolic history of the royal, noble and private families of our country.

It is not until the reign of King Richard I that the arms of the English sovereigns can be authoritatively traced. The arms of King Edward III, in consequence of his claim to be King of France, have on the first and fourth quarters of his shield the lilies of France, and on the second and third quarters three lions. These arms were changed in 1405 in the first and fourth quarters from a semée of lilies to three fleur-de-lis. This coat remained unaltered until the union of the crowns in 1603, when the quarters became 1st and 4th France and England, 2nd Scotland, 3rd Ireland.

In 1707 the arms appointed were 1st and 4th England and Scotland per pale, 2nd France, 3rd Ireland. On the succession of the House of Hanover in 1714 the arms of Hanover were placed in the fourth quarter.

The arms were again altered in 1801, to England in the 1st and 4th quarters, Scotland in the 2nd and Ireland in the 3rd and on an escutcheon of pretence, the shield of Hanover, with an electoral bonnet which in 1816 was changed to a crown. On the accession of Queen Victoria

K

the arms of Hanover were removed from the coat of arms and the present form came into being. Supporters to the shields were introduced in the reign of King Richard II. King Henry VI had two antelopes as supporters. King Edward IV had on the dexter side a lion and on the sinister a white hart, or in some instances a bull.

King Henry VII, as a descendant of the Welsh prince, Cadwallader, had a red dragon on the dexter and a greyhound on the sinister.

The shield of King Henry VIII was supported on the dexter side by a lion and on the sinister by a dragon. King Edward VI had the same supporters. Queen Mary's shield was supported by an eagle on the dexter side and by a lion on the sinister.

Under Queen Elizabeth the lion went to the dexter and on the sinister was a red dragon. On the union of England with Scotland the supporters of the royal arms in England on the dexter side were a lion and on the sinister a unicorn. Since then the supporters have continued the same to the present time.

SOME HERALDIC TERMS

Banner.—The flag of a Knight, containing the quarterings of his arms.

Crest.—The ornament on the top of the helmet, in heraldry placed over the coats of arms.

Cross.—During the Crusades for the recovery of the Holy Land the troops of the various nations displayed crosses on their banners and arms. Every soldier bore a cross upon his dress; the English soldiers adopted the cross of St. George.

Dexter.—That side of a shield which is on the wearer's right—*i.e.* the spectator's left.

Dragon.—An imaginary monster with four legs, a mixture of beast, bird and reptile.

Duke.—The highest degree of British peerage, next below a prince. This title was known in other parts of Europe long before it was introduced into England. The first person that was created a duke in England was Edward the Black Prince, created Duke of Cornwall in 1337 by his father, King Edward III.

Earl.—The third degree of the British peerage.

Escutcheon of pretence.—A small shield superposed on the shield, signifying marriage with an heiress.

Fess.—A horizontal band across the middle of a shield.

Fetterlock.—A handcuff.

Fleur-de-lis.—A conventional representation of the garden lily.

Garter.—The principal badge of the most noble order of the Knights of the Garter: it is worn on the left leg below the knee; it is formed of blue velvet, edged with gold: on the velvet is embroidered the motto of the order, HONI SOIT QUI MAL Y PENSE (Shamed be he who thinks ill of it).

Herald.—Heralds were employed at a very early date as messengers of peace or war; in the time of chivalry as arrangers of tournaments and in more modern times as superintendents of processions, coronations, public ceremonies, and in making proclamations. The office of Garter King at Arms replaced that of Windsor Herald in 1417. Heralds became responsible for the registration of Coats of Arms about that date.

Knights of the Garter.—This is the oldest and most honourable order of Knighthood in Europe : it was founded by King Edward III in 1347 ; it consists of twenty-five Knights, to which are added the princes of the blood royal. The King is the Sovereign of the order and there are also honorary Knights from other countries.

Pale.—A perpendicular band down the middle of the shield.

Mantling.—The drapery used to protect the helmet from stains or rust, and the armour from the heat of the sun.

Martlet.—An imaginary bird said to be without legs.

Portcullis.—A grating suspended by chains, used to defend the entrance to a castle. It was the badge of the houses of Tudor and Beaufort.

Quartered.—A shield divided into four equal parts is said to be quartered.

Semée.—A French word for strewn.

Sinister.—That side of a shield which is on the wearer's left—*i.e.* the spectator's right.

Supporters.—Figures placed on each side of the shield as if to support it. Supporters in English heraldry are granted only to persons included in the rank of nobility, or to Knights Grand Cross of various orders.

Surcoat.—A loose garment worn over the armour of a Knight.

Tournaments.—Combats of honour, in which Knights entered the lists to gain reputation in feats of arms.

Viscount.—A degree below an Earl.

Yale.—A mysterious animal, said to be able to swivel its horns. This animal supported the arms of the Lady Margaret, the mother of King Henry VII.

INDEX
OF PERSONS MENTIONED

LIST OF BOOKS USED

WINDSOR CASTLE. W. St. John Hope.

THE ROYAL GUIDE TO WINDSOR CASTLE. W. St. John Hope.

HISTORY OF WINDSOR CASTLE. J. Pote.

OPENING OF THE COFFIN OF KING CHARLES I. Halford.

THE WOODWORK OF THE CHOIR. Dr. M. R. James, O.M., Provost of Eton.

THE WINDSOR GUIDE. 1804.

TUDOR CHURCH MUSIC. Carnegie Trust. Oxford University Press.

KNIGHTS OF THE GARTER. MSS. Volume I and II.

THE CHOIR STALLS OF ST. GEORGE'S WINDSOR. (*Country Life*, December 24, 1927), by the Dean of Windsor.

THE WOODWORK OF ST. GEORGE'S WINDSOR. (*Country Life*, April 28, 1928), by the Dean of Windsor.

www.ingramcontent.com/pod-product-compliance
Lightning Source LLC
Chambersburg PA
CBHW051841040426
42447CB00006B/645